THE ODDEST
SUPERSTITIONS
OF ALL TIME

THE LEGENDARY
WORLD OF SPORTS

BY WILL GRAVES

SportsZone
An Imprint of Abdo Publishing | abdopublishing.com

abdopublishing.com

Published by Abdo Publishing, a division of ABDO, PO Box 398166, Minneapolis, Minnesota 55439. Copyright © 2016 by Abdo Consulting Group, Inc. International copyrights reserved in all countries. No part of this book may be reproduced in any form without written permission from the publisher. SportsZone™ is a trademark and logo of Abdo Publishing.

Printed in the United States of America, North Mankato, Minnesota
082015
012016

THIS BOOK CONTAINS
RECYCLED MATERIALS

Cover Photo: Mark Ellias/AP Images
Interior Photos: Mark Ellias/AP Images, 1; Denis Poroy/AP Images, 4; Dave Martin/AP Images, 6; Al Messerschmidt/AP Images, 9; Ed Reinke/AP Images, 10; Gerald Herbert/AP Images, 13; Hans Deryk/AP Images, 14; Paul Cannon/AP Images, 16; Leonard Ignelzi/AP Images, 19; Rick Silva/AP Images, 20; Greg Smith/AP Images, 22; Pat Sullivan/AP Images, 24; Richard Drew/AP Images, 26, 34; Ng Han Guan/AP Images, 28; Ella Ling/BPI/Rex Features/AP Images, 30; Mark J. Terrill/AP Images, 32; Matt Slocum/AP Images, 36; Chris Lee/KRT/Newscom, 39; Lacy Atkins/AP Images, 41; Mike Carlson/AP Images, 42; Charles Bennett/AP Images, 45

Editor: Patrick Donnelly
Series Designer: Nikki Farinella

Library of Congress Control Number: 2015945548

Cataloging-in-Publication Data
Graves, Will.
 The oddest superstitions of all time / Will Graves.
   p. cm. -- (The legendary world of sports)
ISBN 978-1-62403-993-5 (lib. bdg.)
Includes bibliographical references and index.
1. Sports--Juvenile literature.   2. Sports--Miscellanea--Juvenile literature.
3. Superstitions--Juvenile literature.   I. Title.
796--dc23
                                                    2015945548

TABLE OF CONTENTS

1 Scarlet Sundays: Tiger's Red Shirt 5

2 Carolina Blue: Jordan's Secret 8

3 Chomping Coaches:
Tark's Towel, Les's Grass 11

4 Goofy Goalies: Fascinating and Focused 15

5 Chicken Tenders: Boggs's Bird Banquet 18

6 Batty Batters: Routine or Rain Delay? 21

7 Baseball Flakes:
Brush Teeth and Turn Left 25

8 What a Racket: Rafa's Routine 29

9 Peculiar Playoffs:
Bad Beards, Trophy Taboo 33

10 Crusty Caps: Baseball's Worst Hats 37

11 Gridiron Goofiness: Football Freaks 40

12 No-Hit Nonsense: Just Say No 43

HONORABLE MENTIONS 46
GLOSSARY 47
FOR MORE INFORMATION 47
INDEX 48
ABOUT THE AUTHOR 48

SCARLET SUNDAYS
TIGER'S RED SHIRT

Tiger Woods was just trying to be a good son. Growing up as one of the world's best young golfers, Woods got a lot of advice. When his mother, Tida, told him he should start wearing red on Sunday, he listened.

"My mom thinks that's my power color," Woods said. "You know you should always listen to your mom."

It worked out pretty well. Sunday is the day when the final round of most golf tournaments is held. Woods has won 14 major championships. And in every picture from the final round of those tournaments, he is wearing a red shirt.

Wearing red on Sunday was Tiger Woods's trademark even before he turned pro.

Tiger Woods tips his cap as he walks up the 18th fairway during the final round of the 2003 Masters.

Woods won the 1997 Masters by a record 12 shots. He won the 2000 US Open by an amazing 15 shots. He pumped his fist after a miracle chip from the fringe on the way to the 2005 Masters title. And he wore a red shirt for the final round every time.

Courses change. Opponents change. Woods's commitment to wearing red does not. It goes back to his time in college. Woods played at Stanford University in California. The school colors at Stanford just happen to be red and white. Woods won the National Collegiate Athletic Association (NCAA) individual title when he was a sophomore.

Woods says he likes knowing what he is going to wear on Sunday. It gives him less to think about as he prepares for the final round. Woods and the people at Nike pick out his outfits a year in advance. He experiments with other colors during the week, including gray and blue.

Just not on Sunday. Sundays are reserved for red.

PAR FOR THE COURSE

Golf is full of strange superstitions, but most of them are hidden. Payne Stewart got rid of the ball if he made a bogey with it. Jack Nicklaus carried three coins in his pocket at all times. Ernie Els throws out the ball after he makes a birdie or better on a hole. He believes each ball has only one good score in it.

2

CAROLINA BLUE

JORDAN'S SECRET

Michael Jordan spent most of his career in the National Basketball Association (NBA) wearing the red of the Chicago Bulls. But he had a very different color hidden beneath his shorts.

Jordan grew up in North Carolina. He went on to have a memorable career at the University of North Carolina. As a freshman, he hit a jump shot in the final seconds to help the Tar Heels beat Georgetown to win the NCAA championship.

The Bulls picked Jordan third overall in the 1984 NBA Draft. He had to trade his beloved Carolina blue for Chicago's black-and-red uniforms. He wanted to stay close to his roots, so he came up with an idea.

Bulls stars Scottie Pippen, *left*, and Michael Jordan helped popularize the baggy-shorts look in the early 1990s.

He would wear his North Carolina shorts under his Bulls shorts.

To make it happen, Jordan had to get creative. He asked the NBA for permission to wear longer shorts. So the league allowed Jordan to wear shorts that were wider and longer than the other players.

Wearing two pairs of shorts did not hurt Jordan's game. He won six NBA titles with the Bulls in the 1990s. He also started a trend. People thought his longer shorts looked so cool that other players started to wear them too. None of them, though, had a second pair underneath.

3

CHOMPING COACHES

TARK'S TOWEL, LES'S GRASS

You might think a towel is for drying off after a dip in the pool or a hot shower. Legendary college basketball coach Jerry Tarkanian had a different reason for bringing a towel to the bench during games.

When Tarkanian was coaching in California in the 1950s, he needed a way to keep his mouth cool on the sideline. During one really hot game, he asked the equipment manager to dip a towel in cold water. When Tarkanian needed to cool off, he put the towel in his mouth.

UNLV coach Jerry Tarkanian gets a mouthful of towel during the 1990 NCAA title game.

Tarkanian liked the way it worked so much that he began to request one wet towel and one dry towel. He would take turns putting each one in his mouth.

Tarkanian's greatest success came at the University of Nevada, Las Vegas (UNLV). The Runnin' Rebels won the NCAA title in 1990. The school built a statue to honor Tarkanian. The statue shows Tarkanian sitting on a bench with a towel between his teeth. His nickname was Tark the Shark. Like a shark, he was—in a way—known for his bite.

Louisiana State University (LSU) football coach Les Miles has a superstition that is a little dirtier. In tense situations during games, Miles likes to reach down and pull up a few blades of grass. That part is not so weird. But then he eats the grass.

Miles says he does it because it keeps him grounded. It reminds him that he is part of the game. And it probably does not spoil his appetite for his postgame meal.

LSU football coach Les Miles sometimes eats grass during games.

4

GOOFY GOALIES
FASCINATING AND FOCUSED

You have to be a little strange to be a hockey goaltender. Who wants to have a rubber puck shot at them at 100 miles per hour (161 kmh)? So it makes sense that many goalies have their own strange superstitions. Patrick Roy won four Stanley Cups in his career with the Montreal Canadiens and the Colorado Avalanche of the National Hockey League (NHL). He also did a bunch of wacky stuff before and during games.

Roy got dressed in the same order every day. He talked to the goal posts. He stepped across the painted red lines and blue lines on the ice instead of

Patrick Roy had a number of quirks, but so what? He won four Stanley Cups.

You might get sick too if—like Glenn Hall, *right*—you had to face the likes of Gordie Howe without a mask.

skating over them. Roy joked that his superstitions got a "little crazy" near the end of his playing days.

Longtime NHL goalie Ed Belfour did not let anybody touch his equipment. And he was not exactly the friendliest guy before the opening faceoff. Belfour focused on his job so intensely that he usually did not talk to his teammates at all.

Glenn Hall made the Hall of Fame for his goaltending skill. If there was a Hall of Fame for stressful pregame routines, he would be in that one too. Hall threw up before every game he played. The ritual started because he was so nervous before games. Then he started to believe that if he did not throw up, he would have a bad game. On those days he would make himself get sick.

Despite his restless nerves, Hall went on to have a great NHL career. He made the All-Star team 11 times in his 18-year career. Hall played in 906 regular-season games and 115 more in the playoffs. That is a lot of trips to the bathroom.

SWEDISH SIPPER

Pelle Lindbergh grew up in Sweden but played goaltender for the Philadelphia Flyers of the NHL. To relax during his games he would sip a Swedish beer called Pripps between periods. He would have the beer with exactly two ice cubes to help keep him cool.

5

CHICKEN TENDERS

BOGGS'S BIRD BANQUET

Wade Boggs's teammates never had to ask him what he was having for his pregame meal. The answer was always the same. While his teammates had pizza or cheeseburgers or meatloaf, Boggs ate chicken every single night.

The Hall of Fame third baseman joked that he was a "chicken-tarian" because he ate so much of it. His teammates just called him Chicken Man. Boggs's pregame meal during his entire 18-year major league career included some version of a chicken dish. Boggs said other meats were too heavy in his stomach. He felt lighter after eating chicken.

His bat looked light in his hands as he smacked the ball all over the field. Boggs racked up 3,010 career

The sweet swing of Wade Boggs was fueled by a daily diet of chicken.

hits and led the American League (AL) in batting average five times in the 1980s. To make sure he did not get bored from always eating the same thing, Boggs experimented with different chicken recipes. He even helped write a cookbook called *Fowl Tips*. The book included all of his favorite chicken recipes cooked by his wife, his mother, and his grandmother.

Boggs did not give up eating chicken once he retired in 1999. He still eats chicken several times a week.

6

BATTY BATTERS
ROUTINE OR RAIN DELAY?

It is said that hitting a baseball is the hardest thing to do in sports. Even the best hitters only reach base on hits 3 times out of 10. No wonder so many players turn to superstitions for a little extra help.

Nomar Garciaparra was one of the best infielders in baseball during his 14-year career. He made the All-Star team six times. He also made pitchers a little bit antsy because of his time-consuming ritual before each pitch.

After every ball or strike, Garciaparra tugged the batting gloves on each of his hands. He was not done. Next he tapped home plate with his bat. He still was

Adjusting his batting gloves was just part of Nomar Garciaparra's routine before every pitch.

Mike Hargrove was known as the Human Rain Delay for his extensive adjustments at the plate.

not done. He then touched the brim of his cap and dug his cleats into the dirt just a little bit deeper.

Garciaparra said he did it because he liked everything feeling "tight." It worked enough for him to win two batting titles and the 1997 AL Rookie of the Year Award.

But Garciaparra had nothing on Mike Hargrove. A first baseman for 12 big-league seasons, Hargrove had one of the most unusual at-bat routines ever seen. After every pitch he stepped out of the batter's box and spent the next 30 seconds or more fidgeting. He would touch his helmet, tug at his shirt, tighten his batting gloves, and tap the dirt off his cleats. Sometimes he would do the entire sequence twice before stepping back into the box. Hargrove earned his nickname—the Human Rain Delay—because his routine took so long.

These time-consuming rituals bothered some opponents. But Garciaparra's teammates wondered if maybe he was on to something.

"If Nomar is superstitious, then maybe more people in the world need to have them," Andre Ethier said. "It works."

7

BASEBALL FLAKES
BRUSH TEETH AND TURN LEFT

A lot of people love licorice, even if it is bad for your teeth. But nobody loved licorice the way Turk Wendell did. In his 11-year career as a major league relief pitcher, Wendell had a few noteworthy quirks. One of them would make a dentist cringe.

Before every inning he pitched, Wendell jammed four pieces of black licorice into his mouth. Then, when the inning was over, he spat the licorice out and brushed his teeth in the dugout. When the next inning started, he would go through the whole routine again.

That was not the only strange thing Wendell did. He would leap over the chalk baseline when walking

Turk Wendell, *right*, slams the rosin bag into the dirt as he prepares to pitch in a 1999 game.

Kevin Rhomberg, *sliding*, was known as one of the most superstitious players in Major League Baseball history.

onto and off the field. He always drew three crosses in the dirt on the back of the mound. And he always waved to the centerfielder before delivering his first pitch of an inning. Wendell's teammates thought he was a little weird. When he started striking out opponents, they learned to get over it.

But Wendell was relatively normal compared to Kevin Rhomberg. He played only 41 games in the majors with the Cleveland Indians in the 1980s. But Rhomberg left a lasting memory. No player in baseball history had as many odd superstitions.

Rhomberg had a rule that if a teammate or a player touched him, he had to touch the player back. So if he was tagged out running the bases, he would chase down the player who tagged him when the inning was over. One time a teammate touched Rhomberg while he was not looking. So Rhomberg went into the dugout and touched every player on the Indians to make sure he got the guy who touched him.

He also refused to make a right turn on the field. His theory was that baseball players should only turn left, like they do when they run the bases. So if he had to turn right, he would instead make three sharp left turns before proceeding. Rhomberg said he knew his quirks were a little weird. But they were part of the routine that helped him become a good ballplayer.

8

WHAT A RACKET
RAFA'S ROUTINE

Rafael Nadal is one of the greatest tennis players ever. The Spanish superstar picked up a few superstitions on the way to the top.

Nadal has won more than a dozen Grand Slam titles. He has also raised a few eyebrows with his unusual daily routine. The rituals begin long before Nadal grabs a racket. He must take a cold shower 45 minutes before his match to get ready. Nadal says the shower helps him get in "the flow."

The flow is just the start. Once Nadal is dressed and ready to go, the rituals pick up speed. He has to carry one racket in his left hand when he walks onto the court. During the coin toss before the match,

Tennis star Rafael Nadal is known for requesting a towel after every point.

Rafael Nadal, *right*, jumps during the coin toss before his match with Roger Federer at the 2014 Australian Open.

he jumps up and down. After the coin toss, he runs to the baseline to begin warming up. He tries to make sure he does not step on the baseline between points, and that he leads his right foot over the line before his left.

Nadal works up quite a sweat when he plays. To keep dry, he asks for a towel after every point, even if he is not sweaty. And between games he sips on his energy drink first, then his water—always in that order. Then he carefully returns both bottles to the same positions.

BORG'S BEARD

Nadal is not the only tennis player to do his own thing. Björn Borg became a legend in the 1970s. Every year before playing at Wimbledon, Borg would grow a beard. He would also wear the same white shirt before every match. It worked well enough for him to win the tournament five straight times.

9

PECULIAR PLAYOFFS
BAD BEARDS, TROPHY TABOO

Hockey players are some of the toughest athletes around. When the NHL playoffs begin, they become some of the hairiest too. Most players ditch their razors and let their facial hair grow until they are knocked out of the playoffs.

The superstition started with the great New York Islanders teams of the early 1980s. The Islanders won four straight Stanley Cups between 1980 and 1983. Every spring when the Stanley Cup playoffs would start, many of the Islanders would stop shaving.

"Everyone just said, 'Hey, that's kind of cool,'" Islanders left wing Clark Gillies said. "So we all started doing it."

Jason Smith did not touch the trophy when the Edmonton Oilers won the Western Conference in 2006.

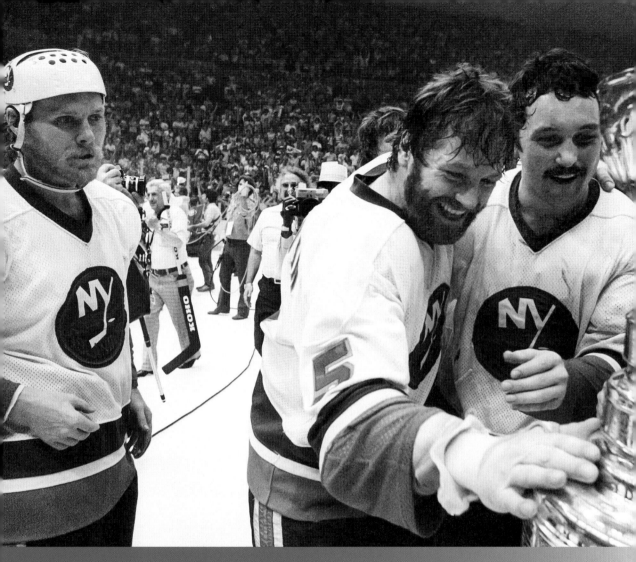

Butch Goring, *left*, and Denis Potvin, *center*, were among the New York Islanders players who grew beards during their Stanley Cup runs of the early 1980s.

The rest of the NHL soon caught on. The playoffs can last up to two months. By the time a champion is crowned, some of the players can look like cavemen.

Others can only grow wispy peach fuzz on their cheeks. But they put up with the razzing of their teammates and fans. They consider it a small price to pay to get their hands on the Stanley Cup.

Speaking of the Cup, it is the only trophy in hockey that many players allow themselves to touch. But you can only touch it if you have won it. Legend has it that a player who touches the Stanley Cup without having won it will never win it.

Some people also consider it taboo to touch the conference championship trophies. The Western Conference winners earn the Clarence Campbell Bowl. The Eastern Conference winners claim the Prince of Wales Trophy. But when the team captain is presented the trophy, he usually will not touch it. Some players believe that if you accept the conference trophy, you will not win the Stanley Cup.

10

CRUSTY CAPS
BASEBALL'S WORST HATS

Fans love a good baseball cap. The best are the kind that fit perfectly on your head. If you are lucky enough to make the major leagues, you can have as many hats as you want.

Pitcher Steve Kline did not need tons of hats. He only needed one. He would pick a hat out in spring training and wear it during the entire 162-game season. He never washed it or gave it a day off. Kline made a decent living as a left-handed relief pitcher in his 11 big-league seasons. His crusty, sweat-stained caps made him famous.

Kline became so well known for his messy hats that the St. Louis Cardinals once held a "Dirty Hat Day." The

Vladimir Guerrero's helmet was covered in so much pine tar it was often hard to read the team logo.

first 5,000 fans at the game went home with a replica dirty hat of their own. Kline finally started putting on clean caps in 2004. But only because Major League Baseball started punishing players for breaking the rules on uniforms.

Kline was not the first player to hold onto a cap with a little dirt on it. Milwaukee Brewers pitcher Mike Caldwell wore the same hat over the final months of the 1982 season. It is easy to see why he did not want to change. Caldwell won seven straight games at one point and the Brewers reached the World Series.

Some position players like their caps clean but their batting helmets messy. Slugger Vladimir Guerrero liked his batting helmet covered in pine tar. It made the helmet look like it was coated with mud. It did not stop Guerrero from smashing homers. He hit 449 homers playing for four teams from 1996 to 2011.

St. Louis Cardinals reliever Steve Kline, shown here in 2004, liked to wear the same hat all season.

11

GRIDIRON GOOFINESS
FOOTBALL FREAKS

Football players usually think they are too tough to get caught up in superstitions. Still, some have come up with their own little routines to help deal with the pressure of the game.

Kicker Ray Wersching helped the San Francisco 49ers win two Super Bowls in the 1980s. He made 222 field goals during his career. He made each one even though he never looked at the goalposts.

Kicking at Candlestick Park in San Francisco was tough. The wind swirled and came from different directions. So Wersching took his mind off the wind by keeping his head down. He would pat his holder, Joe Montana, on the back and stare at the ground until it was time to kick the ball.

Kicker Ray Wersching, *right*, keeps his head down as he follows through on a field goal during Super Bowl XVI in 1982.

Wersching is hardly the only football player to do his own thing. Offensive tackle Jonathan Ogden wore the same pair of blue shorts under his uniform every game. Defensive back Gary Baxter ate a bag of Lay's potato chips before kickoff.

Defensive lineman John Henderson liked to get ready to play by having a team trainer smack his helmet as hard as he could. Henderson said it was like getting the first hit of the game out of the way.

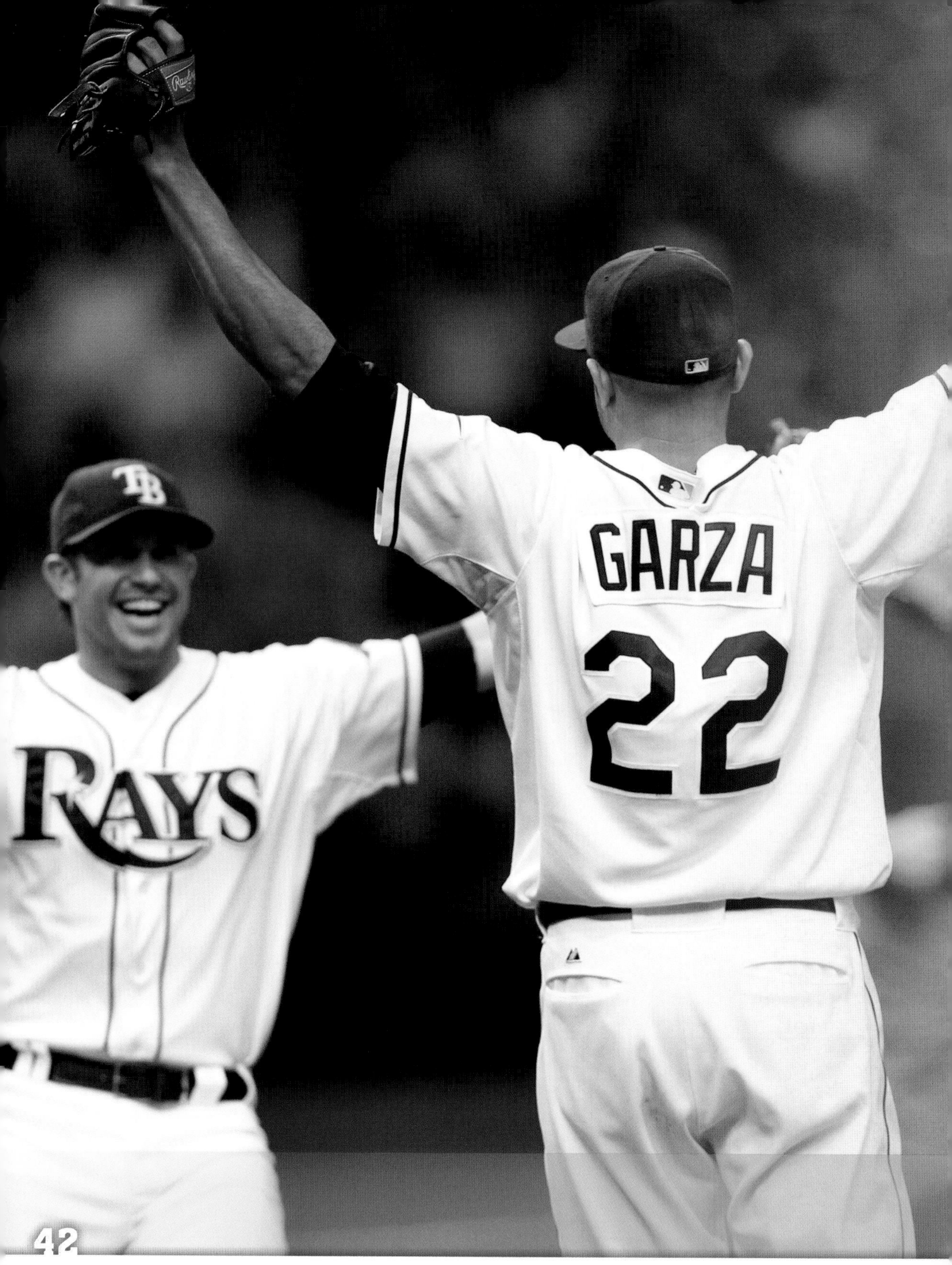
GARZA
22
RAYS
TB

12

NO-HIT NONSENSE
JUST SAY NO

Throwing a no-hitter might be the hardest thing to do in baseball. Imagine going a full nine innings without giving up even one base hit. It sounds impossible. It almost is in the major leagues.

There were only 287 no-hitters thrown between 1876 and 2014. That is about two per season. No-hitters are special games that every player wants to be a part of. They are also usually the best game of a pitcher's career.

Usually a pitcher's teammates will encourage him by letting him know how well he is pitching. But not during a no-hitter. These games bring out one of baseball's oldest superstitions. When a pitcher is

Matt Garza's teammates would not talk to him until after his no-hitter against the Detroit Tigers in 2010.

working on a "no-no," the other guys in the dugout do not talk to him.

For example, Tampa Bay's Matt Garza no-hit the Detroit Tigers on July 26, 2010. As the game wore on, the rest of the Rays players left him alone. Fellow pitcher James Shields did not even get up from his spot on the bench. He worried that if he moved, the Tigers would get a hit. Shields joked that sitting in one spot all night made his behind hurt. But he did it to give Garza a little extra luck.

New York Yankees pitcher Don Larsen threw one of the most famous games in baseball history. Larsen threw a perfect game in the 1956 World Series. That is when a pitcher gets 27 straight outs without a batter reaching base by any means. Larsen tried to chat with teammate Mickey Mantle after the seventh inning. It did not work. When Larsen brought up the perfect game, Mantle got up and walked away.

However, not every player buys into the superstition of not talking about it. Chicago White Sox fans tried to jinx Detroit pitcher Jack Morris in 1984. After every

Jack Morris celebrates after completing his 1984 no-hitter against the Chicago White Sox.

inning the fans would scream at Morris that he was throwing a no-hitter. That was fine by Morris.

"I'm not superstitious," Morris said. "So I hollered back at them and said, 'I know!'"

By the way, Morris got his no-hitter.

HONORABLE MENTIONS

Calling all 3s!—Baseball slugger Larry Walker loved the number 3 so much that he got married on November 3 at 3:33 p.m. He always set his alarm for 33 minutes after the hour.

Chalk Toss—NBA superstar LeBron James used to throw powdered chalk in the air at the scorer's table before every game. He was still doing it during the 2014–15 season, but not before every game.

Follow the Bouncing Ball—Tennis star Serena Williams has a number of superstitions or routines. She always bounces the ball five times before a first serve and twice before a second serve. She has also been known to wear the same pair of socks until she loses a match.

Going Batty—Richie Ashburn, a star outfielder for the Philadelphia Phillies in the 1950s, took no chances with his bats. If he was on a hot streak at the plate, he brought his bats home and slept with them each night.

Nice PJs!—On the night before a game, NBA guard Jason Terry liked to wear the shorts of his team's next opponent.

Oh Baby!—NHL legend Wayne Gretzky used to put baby powder on the blade of his hockey stick before each game. He said it took away some of the stickiness of the tape on the blade.

Sweet Tooth—NFL linebacker Brian Urlacher ate two cookies—preferably chocolate chip—before every game.

Talking Turkey—Minnesota Twins first baseman Justin Morneau won the AL Most Valuable Player Award in 2006. That year, he began stopping at the same sandwich shop and placing the same order—turkey with no sprouts—before every home game.

GLOSSARY

goal posts
Long white or yellow bars standing at the end of a football field.

goaltender
The player in hockey who stays around his team's net and tries to keep the opponents from scoring.

pine tar
A dark, sticky substance used to help baseball players grip their bat handles.

quirk
A peculiar trait or a strange way of acting.

ritual
Something done in the same way or the same order each time.

routine
A regular pattern or way of doing things.

superstition
The idea that doing certain things will bring good or bad luck.

taboo
Forbidden or discouraged due to social customs.

FOR MORE INFORMATION

Books

Gay, Kathlyn. *They Don't Wash Their Socks*. New York: Walker, 2013.

Podnieks, Andrew. *Hockey Superstitions from Playoff Beards to Crossed Sticks and Lucky Socks*. Toronto, Canada: McClelland and Stewart Ltd., 2010.

Wilner, Barry, and Ken Rappoport. *Crazyball: Sports Scandals, Superstitions, and Sick Plays*. Lanham, MD: Taylor Trade Publishing, 2014.

Websites

To learn more about the Legendary World of Sports, visit **booklinks.abdopublishing.com**. These links are routinely monitored and updated to provide the most current information available.

INDEX

Baxter, Gary, 41
Belfour, Ed, 16
Boggs, Wade, 18–19
Borg, Björn, 31

Caldwell, Mike, 38
Candlestick Park, 40
Chicago Bulls, 8–9
Chicago White Sox, 44
Clarence Campbell
   Bowl, 35
Cleveland Indians, 27
Colorado Avalanche, 15

Detroit Tigers, 44–45

Els, Ernie, 7
Ethier, Andre, 23

Garciaparra, Nomar,
   21–23
Garza, Matt, 44
Gillies, Clark, 33
Guerrero, Vladimir, 38

Hall, Glenn, 16–17
Hargrove, Mike, 23
Henderson, John, 41

Jordan, Michael, 8–9

Kline, Steve, 37–38

Larsen, Don, 44
Lindbergh, Pelle, 17
Louisiana State
   University, 12

Mantle, Mickey, 44
Masters Tournament, 6
Miles, Les, 12
Milwaukee Brewers, 38
Montana, Joe, 40
Montreal Canadiens, 15
Morris, Jack, 44–45

Nadal, Rafael, 29–31
New York Islanders, 33
New York Yankees, 44
Nicklaus, Jack, 7
Nike, 7

Ogden, Jonathan, 41

Prince of Wales
   Trophy, 35

Rhomberg, Kevin, 27
Roy, Patrick, 15–16

San Francisco 49ers, 40
Shields, James, 44
St. Louis Cardinals,
   37–38
Stanford University, 6
Stanley Cup, 15, 33–35
Stewart, Payne, 7

Tampa Bay Rays, 44
Tarkanian, Jerry, 11–12

University of Nevada,
   Las Vegas, 12
University of North
   Carolina, 8–9
US Open, 6

Wendell, Turk, 25–27
Wersching, Ray, 40–41
Wimbledon, 31
Woods, Tiger, 5–7

ABOUT THE AUTHOR

Will Graves has been writing about athletes and their weird superstitions for 20 years. Graves has covered everything from the Winter and Summer Olympics to the Kentucky Derby to the NFL, NHL, and MLB playoffs while working for The Associated Press. He's not superstitious but, like Steve Kline, he loves a dirty baseball cap.

discard